# Kitty Cat and the fish

Story by Annette Smith
Illustrations by Ben Spiby

Here comes Kitty Cat.

Kitty Cat is hungry.

Kitty Cat is looking

at the little fish.

Look at Kitty Cat!

"No! No! No!

Kitty Cat, you are naughty!

Go away!"

Kitty Cat runs away.

The little fish are safe.

# Kitty Cat can see Fat Cat.

Fat Cat is looking
at the **big** fish.

Fat Cat's tail
goes up and down,
up and down.

# Here comes Kitty Cat.

"Meow!"

# The **big** fish is safe!